Tick, Tock, Check the Clock!

Lisa Trumbauer
Illustrated by Jackie Urbanovic

A Harcourt Achieve Imprint

www.Rigby.com
1-800-531-5015

Tick, tock,
check the clock.
Hurry, get your sock!

Tick, tock,
check the clock.
Hurry, get your shoe!

Tick, tock,
check the clock.
Hurry, get your bag!

Tick, tock,
check the clock.
Hurry, get your snack!

9

Tick, tock,
check the clock.
Hurry, get your glasses!

Tick, tock,
check the clock.
Hurry, get your ticket!

Tick, tock,
check the clock.

Hurry, get on the plane!